HAUTE COUTURE

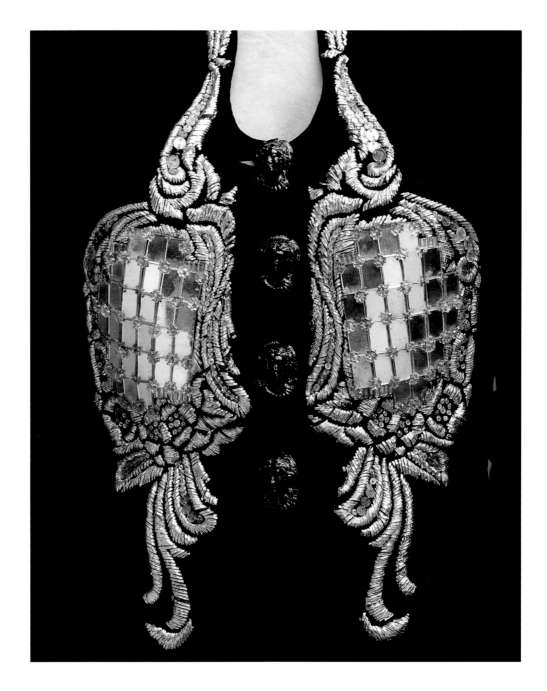

HAUTE COUTURE

RICHARD MARTIN & HAROLD KODA

THE METROPOLITAN MUSEUM OF ART, NEW YORK
DISTRIBUTED BY HARRY N. ABRAMS, INC., NEW YORK

This publication is issued in conjunction with an exhibition held at
The Metropolitan Museum of Art, New York, December 7, 1995–March 24, 1996.

The exhibition is made possible by

CHANEL and **GIANNI VERSACE**

Published by The Metropolitan Museum of Art, New York
John P. O'Neill, Editor in Chief
Barbara Burn, *Executive Editor*
Margaret Aspinwall, *Editor*
Abby Goldstein, *Designer*
Matthew Pimm, *Production Manager*
Robert Weisberg, *Computer Specialist*

All photographs are by Karin L. Willis, the Photograph Studio,
The Metropolitan Museum of Art, except those on pages 17, 20, and 21.

Printed by Meridian Printing Company, East Greenwich, Rhode Island

JACKET/COVER: Jacques Fath. *Ball gown*, ca. 1951 (detail). Black silk velvet with ivory silk satin,
white mink, and gold metal trim. Gift of Mrs. Giorgio Uzielli, 1984 (1984.606.3a,b). See page 85
FRONTISPIECE: Elsa Schiaparelli. Evening jacket, spring 1939 (detail)
Black silk velvet embroidered with gold metal-wrapped thread and mirrors.
Gift of Mrs. Pauline Potter, 1950 (CI 50.34.2)

LIBRARY OF CONGRESS CATALOGING-IN-PUBLICATION DATA
KODA, HAROLD.
Haute couture / by Richard Martin and Harold Koda.
p. cm.
ISBN 0-87099-761-0 (HC)—ISBN 0-8109-6496-1 (Abrams)—ISBN 0-87099-762-9 (pbk. : alk. paper)
1. Costume—History—19th century—Exhibitions. 2. Costume—History—20th century—Exhibitions.
3. Costume—New York (N.Y.)—Exhibitions. 4. Costume Institute (New York, N.Y.)—Exhibitions.
I. Martin, Richard (Richard Harrison) II. Metropolitan Museum of Art (New York, N.Y.) III. Title
NK4709.K63 1995
746.9′2′090340747471—dc20 95-45361
CIP

NOTE: Unless otherwise indicated, the costumes illustrated in this publication are in
the collection of The Costume Institute, The Metropolitan Museum of Art.

CONTENTS

SPONSOR'S STATEMENT

CHANEL and I are honored to contribute to the support of "Haute Couture," the new exhibition at The Costume Institute of The Metropolitan Museum of Art. Coco Chanel in her time did a lot for the arts and even more for the artists.

This "Haute Couture" exhibition, with its treasures of workmanship, design, and grace, will bring to the public the vision of an art that must never be forgotten while constantly evolving as a witness of its period in time.

I am pleased that our support will allow The Costume Institute to present an exciting new perspective on the timeless world of couture.

KARL LAGERFELD

SPONSOR'S STATEMENT

I am extremely pleased to have the opportunity to support an event as momentous as the "Haute Couture" exhibition at The Costume Institute of The Metropolitan Museum of Art. As with other artistic conceptions, a designer's couture collection allows rare insight into a vision of ideal form and expression. Although it may evoke a sense of timelessness, its essence is a reflection of the mood of its particular time and culture.

This exhibition, with the vast resources of The Costume Institute to enrich it, is so important because it will provide the rare occasion to study the fascinating metamorphosis of couture, from its origins to the current movement toward a new simplicity of shape and modernism of fabric and technology. As in the past, today's couture is evolving in recognition of its time. As we approach the millennium, I passionately believe that the innovations of couture will continue to set the modern standards of clothing design. As such, I offer praise and applause to the Metropolitan Museum for its vision in presenting a study in haute couture.

GIANNI VERSACE

Detail of Chanel evening gown (see page 96)

FOREWORD

Haute couture, fashion's art of supreme technical mastery and virtuoso execution, is handsomely and perhaps peerlessly represented in the collection of The Costume Institute of The Metropolitan Museum of Art. This book and the exhibition it accompanies present the historical landmarks of couture and also the persistent discrimination and authority of high aesthetic quality that characterize it.

One of a suite of exhibitions examining the Museum's collections, it brings the same principles of connoisseurship and careful visual examination and judgment to the art objects of fashion that are used to address other visual arts, although in this area we are not bound to discern the authentic and reject the lesser. Without question, the fine arts have a correspondence in haute couture, the specific art of fashion that begins in the same generation as modern art. As we examine these couture garments in this exhibition and in these pages, we enjoy the discriminating details that disclose the privileges of craft and visual acumen. We can look at feathers partially stripped and sewn together to achieve an effect unmatched in nature, and at sequining that displays the multiple treatments of metal, bead, or stone transfigured to a shimmering surface. We can see mundane materials maneuvered with the proficient and perfecting skills of haute couture to become unequivocally beautiful garments. And we can appreciate with the connoisseur's gratification the illusions of trompe l'oeil and the secret satisfactions of handsewn detail unmatched in conventional dress.

The exhibition is made possible by financial support from Chanel and Gianni Versace, and to them we give most appreciative thanks for their generosity.

That the costumes chosen to illustrate the finest moments and outstanding examples of haute couture are almost all from the collection of The Costume Institute is due to the donors who have bestowed on us gifts of the most important and most impressive clothing ever made. We are grateful to them, as we are also to the lenders to the present exhibition. This selection magnificently illustrates fashion's highest ambitions and our belief in costume as a compelling constituent of visual culture.

PHILIPPE DE MONTEBELLO
Director, The Metropolitan Museum of Art

INTRODUCTION

In a story, perhaps apocryphal, Diana Vreeland commanded an assistant going to Paris just after World War II to bring her back an artificial rose made for the adornment of the haute couture. By the quality of such a token would Vreeland know that artisanry and commitment remained in the creations of Paris. Satisfied with her 1940s rose, Vreeland knew that the couture was renascent after the war.

For more than a century, the couture has been emblem of the triumph of costume and fashion. It represents the fusion of fashion—the modern entity composed of novelty and synergy with personal and social needs—and costume—the consummate arts of dressmaking, tailoring, and constituent crafts to apparel and accessories. Founded in the crucible of modernism's invention in the middle years of the nineteenth century in Paris, with the expanded patronage cultivated by the House of Worth, but still dependent upon the considerable support of Empress Eugénie, the couture has long stood as the modern equilibrium between the garment as exquisite aggregate and the burgeoning notions of fashion as a system.

This exhibition is created around the collection of The Costume Institute, rich in the germinal and indicative pieces of the haute couture. Perhaps nowhere else in the world is there assembled a collection so fully demonstrative of the haute couture. Thus we have chosen to show the couture in two principal aspects. The outline of the history of modern dress can be presented in the extraordinary examples of the haute couture offered here. And one can see the constituent skills both in the couture house for dressmaking and for tailoring and in adjunct workshops for related skills and ornament.

The legend of Vreeland's rose also suggests the heartfelt faith in the couture. The dove returning with an olive branch to Noah's ark could hardly have been more welcome. The persistence of the haute couture is as roundly questioned and doubted and debated as the survival of painting or the supposed death of Broadway. These conventions that stand for more than their arts themselves have become signs for art's survival. Some may have doubted that the couture would survive its founder, the entrepreneurial Charles Frederick Worth, and the periodic upheavals of the 1870s and 1880s. In the early years of the twentieth century, Paul

Poiret took couture into an admittedly dangerous path of change, responding to Orientalist and social sirens, but even more to the beckoning of commerce and the use of the couture as a generating engine for fashion and fragrance broadly disseminated. Initially, Poiret's self-conscious avant-gardism was attacked by the House of Worth as not meriting the haute couture tradition that Worth embodied, but a progressive novelty-driven century was perhaps inexorable. As the couture of the 1930s expanded, those who could actually make garments chose to disparage those who could only sketch or otherwise envision them, setting off a classic battle of conceptual art versus technical proficiency that is also a sign of the century in myriad arts.

Even Vreeland's rose is a couture story couched in the circumstances of the other visual arts. After all, the school of Paris vis-à-vis the fine arts had more or less decamped during the war; one would not have found the same reassurance, other than the already venerable figures of Picasso, Braque, and Matisse, in the world of painting and sculpture. Vreeland's test of the rose is, of course, a synecdoche, but one that makes good sense in a field in which the endeavor of the haute couture is to make the consummate garment, engaging the many perfect crafts that constitute dress. If the skills of the rose were not renewed, there could be no beautiful dress. Matisse, nearly blind and functioning with scissors and colored papers, could create a masterpiece in the artist's sublime autonomy. The couture's version thereof required not only the designer's leadership and will, but the capability of an echelon of *petites mains* proficiencies that stood behind the designer.

Ironically, the couture flourished in the postwar period, beginning with the immense popular appeal of Christian Dior's "New Look" in 1947. Given its name not by Dior, but by the American editor and journalist Carmel Snow, who enthused of the 1947 collection that Dior had given "a new look," this supposed fashion novelty was so successful in part because it knew acutely its history and reconvened the finest skills to the couture. In the economically puissant years of the late 1940s and 1950s, the rebirth of the couture, supported by many American clients and thus well represented in The Costume Institute, was a significant connection between the world of the American century and the couture tradition. To the surprise of those who might have expected the couture to fail in these critical years, it flourished. Even in the 1960s, as the sea changes of the postindustrial society swept the globe and pushed a tide of social exchange, the couture remained in place as a guiding light of fashion. It secured firmly the possibilities established long before by Paul Poiret, Gabrielle Chanel, and Jean Patou of allowing the resonances of couture design to provide an economic structure for the practices of the couture. The supposed détente of the couture in the turbulent years of the late 1960s and 1970s has proved not to be the demise of the artform, but its perdurable system, annexing popular visual culture and exploiting popular successes.

Some have been tempted in the 1990s to forecast the decline and demise of the couture once again. The prophecy is, by historical judgment, improbable. In an epoch of straitened economic circumstances and shaken belief in clothing consumption, all fashion is scrutinized. But the couture's offering of distinction in design and technique remains a compelling force, one even more potent when much other quality has atrophied. Like all the visual arts, the haute couture has evolved in the past hundred years, but it seems no more headed to extinction than the medium that Mondrian made absolute or the forms that Brancusi distilled. On the contrary, the haute couture is headed unabashedly by its own aspirations toward distinction, and in that we have a torch in dim times. That, particularly in 1995, there has been a keen interest in observing the haute couture is testimony to the couture as a force of inspiration. Globally, the excitement about the rediscovery of impeccable tailoring and the possibilities of tastefully splendid clothing in garish times is inevitably led once again by the haute couture, not intending to be sovereign or dictatorial, as it once was, in directing all fashion standards, but in setting an example by which our visual culture would be galvanized and rendered accountable to quality commensurate with our culture at its best.

Today, the haute couture is neither haughty nor superannuated. It is an aesthetic essay in which cherished and extraordinary skills continue to be practiced in service of a late modern age. It remains a discipline of ultimate imagination, unaccountable to cost, with the paradox of being the fashion most cognizant of its ideal clients. It is, as it began, a dream of quality in an era of industry and its succession. The haute couture persists in providing us with a paragon of the most beautiful clothing that can be envisioned and made in any time.

HISTORY

The history of the haute couture begins with two extraordinary circumstances. Its founder is Charles Frederick Worth, an Englishman, though its city of destiny always is Paris. The haute couture was founded in the same epoch in which the sewing machine was invented. In the face of a growing technology, an art of hand-sewn techniques arose in order to establish a distinction affiliated with an old order. What had been the particular skills of dressmaking and tailoring in the service of individual clients, and in a few instances to some partially assembled or ready-to-wear garments, became an independent enterprise, one that answered to clients but took its initiative from the concepts of the fashion designer, now no artisan to the state or patron, but a viably independent creator.

Further, that the haute couture arose in the same place and time as modern art in the context of Manet and Baudelaire cannot be mere coincidence. The spectatorship and new public that mandated a transfigured art also required a new fashion intended not for court minglings, but for the visible exchanges of boulevards, opera houses, even cafés. The history of the haute couture is, from inception, closely aligned to the history of modern art. The expressive opulence of nineteenth-century dress, familiar in paintings of the period by such fashion-acute observers as Manet, Degas, and Seurat, rendered the visual spectacle that captivated the modern movement in its interest in urban life and the emotional life of individuals. The shapes that evolved from Worth's original crinoline bubbles were perhaps always structures seeking the effortless lightness of modernity that Worth had seized so instinctively in the 1850s and 1860s.

Like Cubism's and Futurism's assertive fracturing of the world, the haute couture was dramatically challenged and changed in the first decades of the twentieth century. Like every other phenomenon of the century, the haute couture bifurcated into conservative and avant-garde strands in the beginning of the century, only to be reunited in the 1970s. This schism, deliberately precipitated by Paul Poiret after he was dismissed by the House of Worth, has forced as many misreadings of fashion as it has in other visual arts. It is hard to describe Callot Soeurs as either conservative or radical, so thoroughly combined and compatible are the traits of each pole. Likewise, it would be hard to think of Jeanne Lanvin without her edgy, ambitious, advanced aspect, but it is equally true that she practiced a certain etiquette, just as Duchamp's radicalism was accompanied by a dandy and intellectual manner not always associated with aesthetic insurrection. Poiret's prideful invention of novel shapes, depending on the Orientalist conventions of wrapping the body more or less as a pliable cylinder, took the same aggressive position of Cubism's reconstitution of the visual world into a primacy of shapes already sapiently observed by the previous generations of artists. Poiret appended to the haute couture a possibility of extreme novelty and avant-garde positioning, whether in the surprise of a mannequin parade as prototype to the fashion runway show or the reshaping of attire with the boast that he had eliminated the long tyranny of the corset. But an art that speculates in the visual world and that casts itself into the roles of seeing and being seen in that world never forsakes its conserving, socializing options even as the possibility emerges for advanced forms and conceptual ambition.

Thus, the abiding equivocation of twentieth-century couture between convention and change conforms to the positions of art in the same time. Explorations and innovations by Madeleine Vionnet, Jeanne Lanvin, Gabrielle Chanel, and others are sponsored by the artist's objectives and needs, whether arising from dressmaking and tailoring or from the social needs of dress. No designer has been wholly conceptual or wholly artisanal. When formal principles held primacy, the social congress effected through clothing was never completely absent. Chanel's delight in the process and practices of the haute couture may have been secondary to her compelling picture of society, but both principles were effective in her clothing. Similarly, Alix Grès exemplified the sculptor absorbed in technique but was inevitably in the thrall of 1920s and 1930s neoclassicism and the contemporary imagery of powerful women. Elsa Schiaparelli's Surrealism may be an expropriated art, whereas Vionnet's art is fathomed within the garment structure, yet each discovers her individual art of dress.

In the dialectic between Christain Dior and Cristobal Balenciaga in the postwar years, there is a similar disparity in sensibility, despite each designer's profound sense of the couture as an art. One designer's courtly sense of the feminine sublime and the other's robust sensibility for a new swagger and self-confidence guaranteed work that was distinctive but curiously complementary. As art would willingly move from the empyrean of abstraction to the commercial cacophony in the 1960s, so fashion directed itself increasingly to the powerful energy of popular culture. But popular culture and art only proved to fuel the excitement of the haute couture, with the ingenuity of such designers as Pierre Cardin and Yves Saint Laurent appropriating the most contemporary and even seemingly disestablishment gestures into the couture.

PIERRE-LOUIS PIERSON

Countess Castiglione, 1860s
Albumen silver print from
glass negative
David Hunter McAlpin Fund,
1975 (1975.548.116)

The birth of the couture was
attended by infants photography
and modern art. Virginia Oldoini,
Countess Verasis de Castiglione,
was a voracious client of the
couture and photography, acquiring
fashion from the new *maisons de
couture* of Worth and Pingat. For

the new court-affiliated women of
power, as well as the soaring
bourgeoisie, the three arts provided
a new world of spectatorship and
self-satisfaction. The altered image
further suggests the client's
intervention.

CHARLES FREDERICK WORTH

Ball gown, ca. 1887 (left)
Pale green and ivory silk satin, and
yellow, pink, and ivory silk chiffon
with embroidered sunburst pattern
Gift of Orme Wilson and
R. Thornton Wilson, in memory
of their mother, Mrs. Caroline
Schermerhorn Astor Wilson, 1949
(49.3.28a,b)

Ball gown, ca. 1892 (right)
Pink silk damask with crystal
embroidery
Gift of Orme Wilson and
R. Thornton Wilson, in memory
of their mother, Mrs. Caroline
Schermerhorn Astor Wilson, 1949
(49.3.25a,b)

In instances of the elaborate
patterns *à la disposition*, woven to
ultimate configuration as a dress,
the House of Worth created with
great invention. Moreover, the textile is so rich and dense that the
couturier has allowed the selvage,
as thick as grosgrain ribbon, to be
its own finish, embellished with
bullion and embroidery (see detail).
In this decision, the couture garment expresses a startling truth to
its process yet without mitigating
its sumptuous effect.

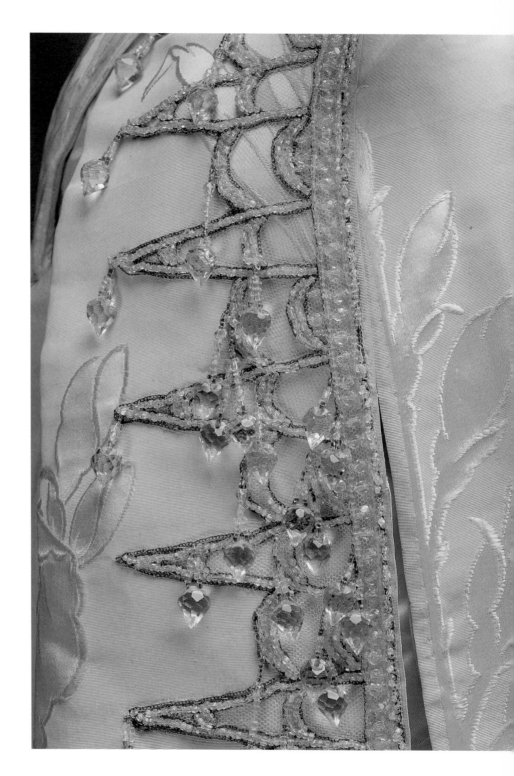

PAUL POIRET

"Sorbet" gown, 1913
Ivory and black silk satin with
seed-beaded appliqués
Courtesy Hope B. McCormick
Costume Center, Chicago Historical
Society, Gift of the Costume
Committee

In the braggadocio of claiming to
liberate women from the corset,
Poiret factually overstated his role
but realized the importance of his
modernization of the clothing
ethos. Influenced by the Orientalism of the 1910s, Poiret took
unstructured lengths of fabrics and
wrapped them around the body in
flagrant opposition to Edwardian
structure and tailored formation.
This detail is a signature Poiret
rose; its finesse is apparent in the
caviar-size seed beads applied to
backing and appliquéd to the dress.

Georges Lepape, *Laquelle?*, plate 5 in *Gazette du
Bon Ton*, September 1913. Courtesy Hope B.
McCormick Costume Center, Chicago Historical
Society, Gift of the Costume Committee

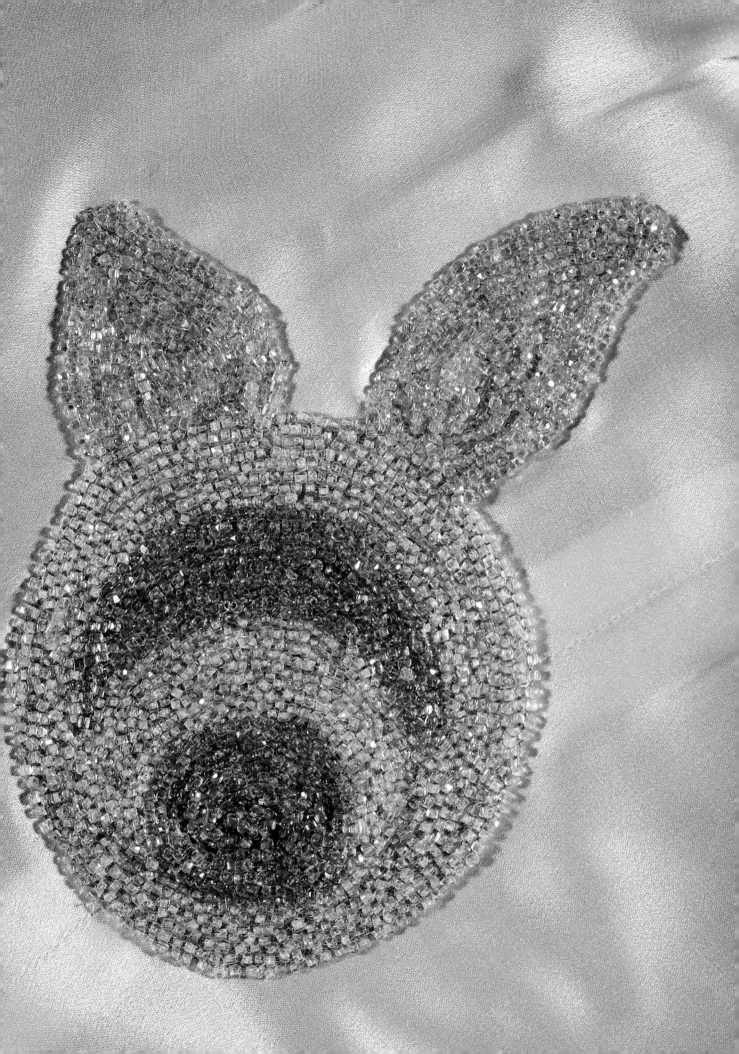

CALLOT SOEURS

Evening gown, 1910–14
Beige cotton net embroidered
with gold, silver, pink, and
copper sequins and beads
The Jacqueline Loewe Fowler
Costume Collection, Gift of
Jacqueline Loewe Fowler, 1981
(1981.380.2)

Attuned to the Orientalism of the
decade, the Callot Soeurs reined the
silhouette to a cylindrical wrap,
effortless in lingerie-weight fabric.
Yet for its innovations, the work of
the Callot Soeurs does not stint the
couture's roster of technical skills.
Here, sequins vary: some are
punched into a filigree pinwheel,
others are hammered flat; in some
instances metal is overlaid onto
faceted crystal (see detail on page
14). But even this ornamentation
is not entirely for the pleasure of
heterogeneity, but for the calculated
and magical effects of such varied
surfaces seen in evening and candle
lights.

JEANNE LANVIN

Robe de style, 1924–25 (left)
Ivory and black silk taffeta
trimmed with pink and black
silk velvet rosettes
Gift of Mrs. W. R. Grace,
1956 (CI 56.49.1)

Robe de style, 1924–25
(right)
Ivory and black silk
taffeta trimmed with pink
and black silk velvet rosettes
Gift of Mrs. William B.
Given Jr., 1979 (1979.122.1)

High art, and haute couture
with it, has often been erro-
neously associated with the
sovereign disposition. But
haute couture has also been
conditioned on the relationship between couture ideas
and the will of the client. A
client seeking a demure
profile might ask for one
décolletage treatment,
while another might
demand an alternative.
A designer would
allow variation only
in modules, but a
couture garment
often becomes a
synergy of client
and couturier.

EDWARD MOLYNEUX

Evening dress, 1926–27
Cream silk georgette embroidered
with iridescent paillettes
Gift of Mrs. Adam Gimbel, 1942
(CI 42.33.3)

The flapper dresses of the 1920s
coexisted in couture and ready-to-
wear, the latter often gaudy, the
former continuing the linear inter-
ests of high-style dress of the
1910s. Molyneux was a modernist
designer of consummate good taste,
walking a fine line between the
refinements of couture style and a
modernist aesthetic and the ambition to be socially and culturally
advanced in the age of Anita Loos
and Gatsby. Sequins in vertical
stripes are overlaid with loose
lengths of georgette picoted along
the edges for a delicate shimmer on
vertical filaments.

Gabrielle Chanel

Day ensemble, 1926
Black wool jersey and silk satin
Purchase, Gift of New-York Historical Society,
by exchange, 1984 (1984.28a–c)

The "little black dress," archetype of clothing's penchant
for social reversal and political change, assumes the
hitherto plebeian material of jersey as a plausible field
for genteel finishing. In all of its layered details, a simple
material becomes elegant through superior technique:
the binding, pleating, and hemming of the skirt, and the
hand-sewn belt epitomize the poverty de luxe, a luxury
most keenly felt amid penury.

Chanel's similar appropriations from riding habits and
menswear demonstrate the same penchant to find utility
and to refine the practical motif through exemplary
execution. As she borrowed such apparel aspects, she inevitably brought the aura of the original association—
even the service uniform—as a frisson to the new use.

MADELEINE VIONNET

Evening gown, 1936–37
Black silk satin with faux ivory
belt buckle
Gift of Madame Madeleine
Vionnet, 1952 (CI 52.18.2)

Vionnet exposed her composition
with characteristic subtlety. The
wide cylinder of bias cut is pulled
in at center front, radiating from
and anchored by the buckle (see
detail). To the casual observer, the
effect is superficial and the buckle
may seem applied decoration. Stra-
tegically placed at the nexus of bias
construction, the center front is the
dynamic convergence of the dress
as a composition. In such a gesture,
Vionnet was a dauntless modernist.

ELSA SCHIAPARELLI

Suit, 1938
Navy blue wool
Gift of Mrs. J. R. Keagy, 1974
(1974.338.1a,b)

While Schiaparelli was herself not
a tailor and was scorned by arch-
rival Chanel for her lack of skills,
she presided over one of the great
tailoring ateliers responsible for the
definitive broad-shouldered and
formfitting suits and jackets of the
1930s. The designer's conceptual
embellishments were based on
this tailoring foundation. In some
instances, the tailors spoke for
themselves, as in this example,
a suit with breast pockets incorporated into the dimension of
the bust.

JEAN PATOU

Suit, ca. 1937
Black wool gabardine with silk
grosgrain inserts
Gift of Mrs. Stephen M. Kellen,
1978 (1978.165.20a,b)

Patou constructed a tailored suit as
if it were a jigsaw puzzle. Formed
as a gabardine suit with all the
pattern pieces wholly constructed,
the silk grosgrain diamonds were
inserted, replacing gabardine
squares. Each diamond is composed
of four mitered elements. By this
analytical technique, the suit is
integrally conceived, and the front
of the suit reveals the wool ground
as a full surround.

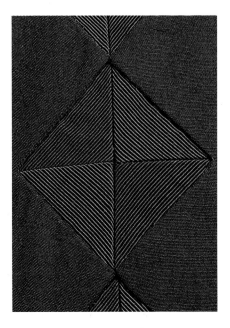

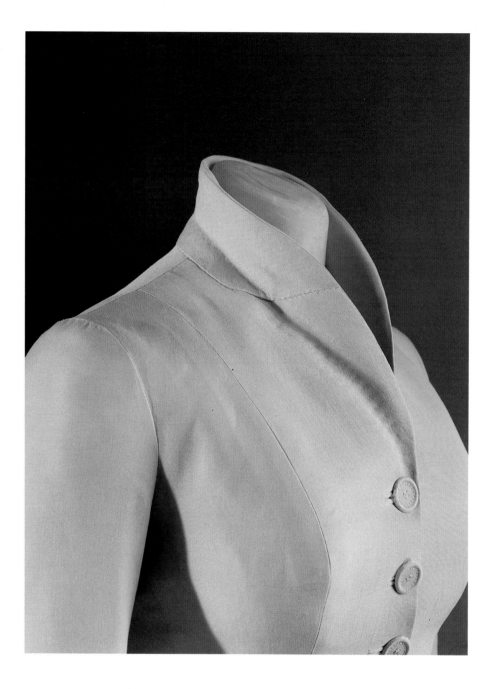

CHRISTIAN DIOR

"Bar" suit, spring 1947
Beige silk jacket with black
wool skirt
Jacket: Gift of Mrs. John Chambers
Hughes, 1958 (CI 58.34.30)
Skirt: Gift of Christian Dior, 1969
(CI 69.40)

The triumph of Dior's "New Look"
was to restore Paris after World
War II as the sovereign city of fashion. Reportedly, Diana Vreeland,
then of *Harper's Bazaar*, asked a
young colleague visiting in Paris
just after the war to bring back a
silk rose of the couture. Seeing the
beauty of that rose, Vreeland
acknowledged that Paris was
revenant. Thus, not only the aura
of glamour was restored, but also
the artisanry that might be
appreciated by a connoisseur of
fine clothing. Symbol of the new,
the Dior "Bar" suit also reveals
the hand stitching at the inside
of the collar and hand-stitched
self-covered buttons of the
atelier *tailleur*.

CRISTOBAL BALENCIAGA

Day dress, 1955–56
Dark brown wool jersey
Gift of Mrs. William Rand, 1964
(CI 64.4.3)

In the 1950s, as the couture made
fashion news and mandates,
Balenciaga achieved leadership
status in mid-decade with the
chemise. While still structured, but
floating over the body, the fluid
effect of the chemise became in
Balenciaga's exaggeration the sack
dress, forsaking the waist and
anticipating the 1960s shift.

In conceiving the chemise,
Balenciaga applied lessons of
suppleness he had long employed
in his collars. Inspired by the
kimono collar, he created a distinctive bias roll collar pushed back
from the neck. In integrating this
collar with the chemise silhouette,
he pitched the amplitude front and
back, allowing the yielding, floating
form of the collar to complement
the softness of the dress.

YVES SAINT LAURENT

"Mondrian" day dress, fall 1965
Red, blue, white, yellow, and black
wool jersey
Gift of Mrs. William Rand, 1969
(CI 69.23)

As the sack dress evolved in the
1960s into a modified form, the
shift, Saint Laurent realized that
the dress's planarity was an ideal
field for color blocks. Knowing the
flat planes of the 1960s canvases
achieved by contemporary artists
in the lineage of Mondrian, Saint
Laurent made the historical case for
the artistic sensibility of his time.
Yet he also demonstrated a feat of
dressmaking, setting in each block
of jersey, piecing in order to create
the semblance of the Mondrian
order and to accommodate the body
imperceptibly by hiding all the
shaping in the grid of seams.

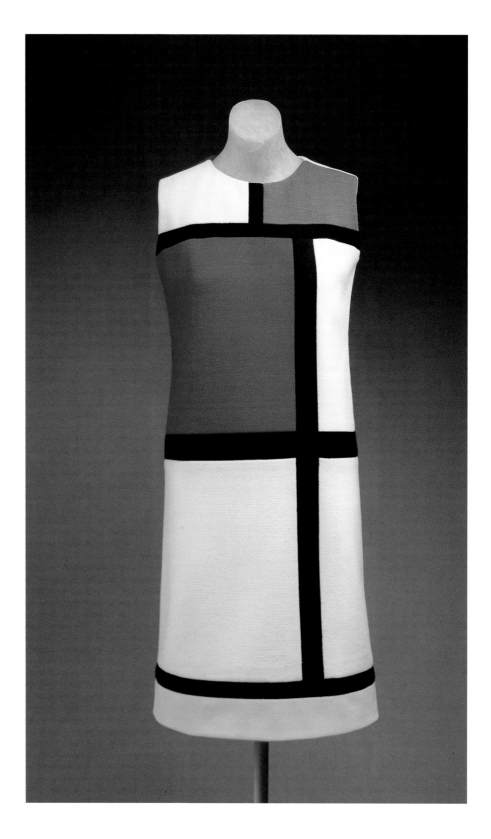

ANDRÉ COURRÈGES

Day ensemble, 1965 (left)
White and red wool and
nylon knit
Gift of Kimberly Knitwear Inc.,
1974 (1974.136.9a,b)

Day dress, 1965 (right)
White wool twill with black silk
grosgrain trim
Gift of Kimberly Knitwear Inc.,
1974 (1974.136.3)

Developing from his training
and sensibility achieved at
Balenciaga, Courrèges applied
the surgical cut and strict tailoring to the geometric planes of
1960s fabric. The thrown-back
rolled collar derives from
Balenciaga, as does a respon-
siveness to comfort. While
attuned to fashion of the very
young as inspired by Mary
Quant and Pierre Cardin,
Courrèges retained Balenciaga's
flattering attention to the
details that obscure age.

ANDRÉ COURRÈGES

Evening dress, 1965
White cotton and green silk
satin completely embroidered
with iridescent sequins
Gift of Jane Holzer, 1974
(1974.384.10)

The paradox of the couture of
the 1960s was its Utopian
dream, tempered by the Space
Age, and its thorough reliance
on traditional techniques.
Thus, Courrèges evokes with
sequins a futuristic suit of
mail disposed between medi-
eval history and speculation
on clothing for the future.
When ready-to-wear fashion
imitated the effects of such
couture, suppleness was often
sacrificed, as was the Utopian
vision of a clothing at once
opulent and optimistic.

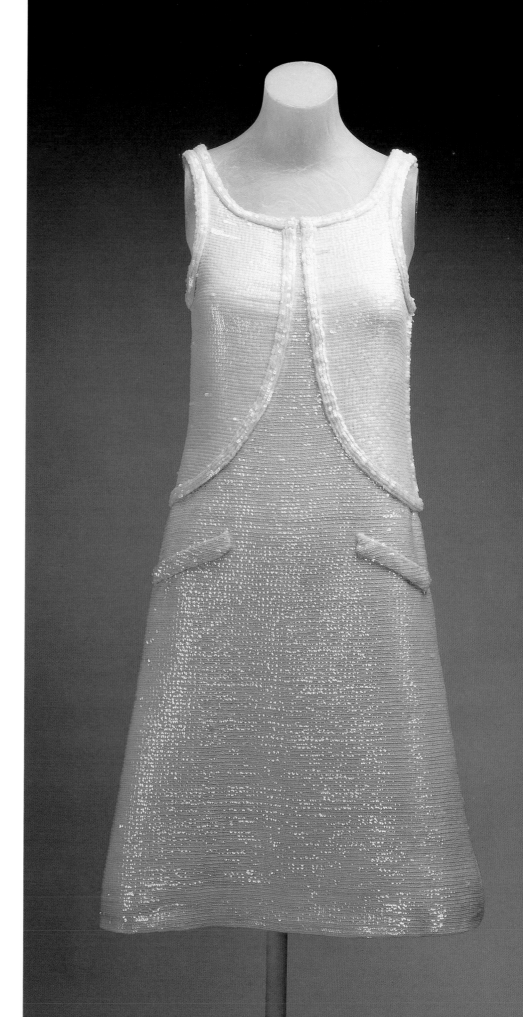

EMANUEL UNGARO

Ensemble, 1969
White elasticized net with allover
appliqués of white braid trefoils
Gift of Mrs. Leonard Holzer, 1970
(1970.89.1a–c)

As fashion's last absolute decree
entered its concluding phase, skirts
became shorter and shorter until
they atrophied into short shorts, or,
in the phrase of the day, hot pants.
In a couture playsuit with matching leggings, the elastic fabric has
been hand-appliquéd with white
braid. In the youth-impassioned
tumult of the time, there was
equivocation between Warhol
superstar and couture client. As
self-consciously insurrectionist as
the political gesture is, the craft of
the garment is, like Chanel's "little
black dress," traditional.

YVES SAINT LAURENT

Pantsuit, 1970 (left)
Brown wool gabardine
Gift of Mireille Levy, 1984
(1984.163.4a,b)

CHRISTIAN DIOR
BY MARC BOHAN

Suit, 1970 (right)

Brown and white wool tweed
Gift of Mireille Levy, 1991
(1991.34.1a–c)

Almost immediately, the response
to very short length in the late
1960s was the militant dropping of
the length to below the knee, graz-
ing the upper calf, and the effective
avoidance of all skirt-length
determinations in pantsuits. The
long-length maxi proved, in its
lack of success, to be a trauma to
the couture, becoming a challenge
to the supposed ultimate authority
of fashion. The maxi was the last
fashion rule; pantsuits—and
cognate menswear borrowings—
survived to constitute the
revolution and resolution of
late-1960s fashion.

YVES SAINT LAURENT

Evening ensemble,
fall/winter 1976–77 (left)
Red silk chiffon with gold stripes,
green silk faille, red silk taffeta
Gift of Bernice Chrysler Garbisch,
1979 (1979.329.6a–d)

Evening ensemble,
fall/winter 1976–77 (right)
Red silk crepe, red silk faille,
green silk taffeta
Gift of Bernice Chrysler Garbisch,
1979 (1979.329.7a–c)

Fashion design in the early 1970s
was dominated by ready-to-wear
and sportswear, both because of
new standards of casual behavior
and because of the expanded
interest of the bourgeoisie in
fashion. In this climate, in which
some mistook the couture's renewed synergy with popular
fashion design as its demise, Saint
Laurent created a reactionary
collection intended to revive the
couture, using the most luxurious
fabrics, feathered turbans, passe-
menterie ties, and horsehair-braid–
reinforced petticoats. Saint Laurent
refreshed the couture, making it
seem desirable and distinctive in a
time of ready-to-wear leadership.
Acclaimed by the *International
Herald Tribune* as "a revolution"
and "the most dramatic and expen-
sive show ever seen in Paris," Saint
Laurent's Russian collection of
fall/winter 1976–77 was counter-
revolutionary to the 1960s.

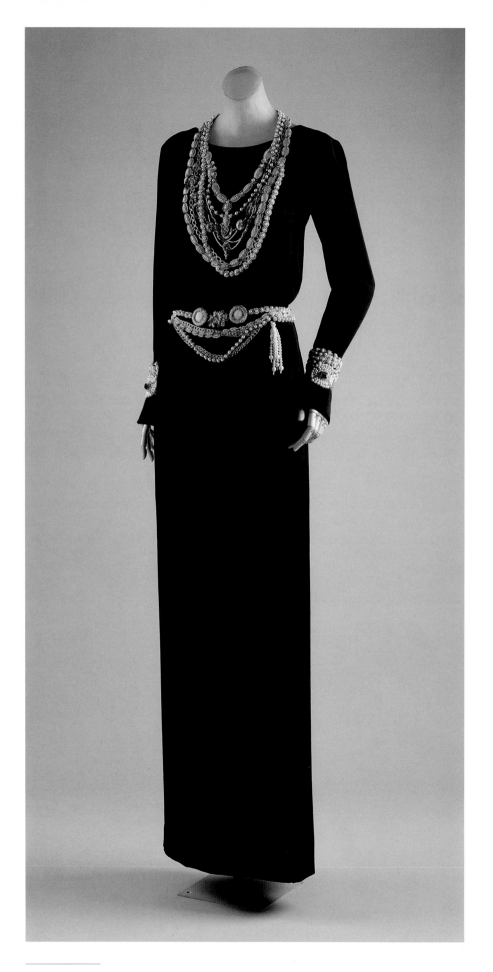

CHANEL
BY KARL LAGERFELD

Trompe l'oeil evening gown, 1983
Black silk with multicolored
beads and gilt embroidery
Courtesy Chanel

In his first collection for the house
of Chanel, Lagerfeld demonstrated
his respect for the tradition of the
designer and his special capacity to
bring new animation to the design.
Playing on Chanel's favored look
and her mingling of real and costume jewelry, Lagerfeld created a
tour de force of jewelry impression,
integrating the embroidered like-
ness of jewelry into the dress.

PATOU
BY CHRISTIAN LACROIX

One-shouldered evening gown,
spring/summer 1987
Raspberry silk taffeta
Gift of Comtesse Thierry de Ganay,
1994 (1994.278)

While lastingly known for his
eighteenth-century–inspired pouf
dress, Lacroix made the most
inflated version of the dress only
when he was the designer for
Patou. There and at his own house,
Lacroix combines luxury and in-
souciance, enamored as he is of all
the artisanal trades, fringe, bead,
embroidery, etcetera. The opulence
of Lacroix is attained by his strong
sense of vibrant color and pattern
mix exacerbated by his willingness
to call in all the opportunities of
couture technique.

GIANNI VERSACE

Evening gown, 1995
Nacreous polyvinyl chloride and
clear vinyl
Courtesy Versace

Like the Chanel "little black dress,"
in which mundane materials are
transformed by couture handwork,
the Versace gown finesses
industrial-weight vinyl into a
crystalline overskirt evocative of
nineteenth-century silhouette, but
realized as a Crystal Palace of
twentieth-century material. To
manipulate the cumbersome vinyl
with the handwork of the couture
is a self-imposed challenge to
merge new technology and old
technique.

ATELIER

The couture house is customarily composed of two parts, one devoted to dressmaking *(flou)*, the other devoted to tailoring *(tailleur)* of suits and coats. The designer is often aided by a *modéliste,* a second in command of design, who works with both ateliers and in particular with fabric suppliers. Skilled workers in each area practice the arts apposite to the area. Embellishment and accessories are added incrementally as applied decoration, often from sources outside the couture house. However, with regard to the unembellished garment, the modern couture house is a completely autonomous workroom of dedicated ateliers. In fact, surprisingly, in view of the elegant locations of most couture houses, the creation of the garments occurs in the *maisons particulières* of the house, thus under the daily surveillance of the designer as well as in intimate connection with the *vendeuses* and other managing personnel. Depending upon the designer, the design process might begin either with sketches or with a muslin or toile, draped and cut.

The skills of the couture that are in the house are essential to its creation. Each part of the atelier has a *première d'atelier* who works to translate the sketch or toile to a finished design. Traditionally, each atelier had a rigorous hierarchy of first hands, second hands, and apprentices. Only the first hands have conventionally been allowed to work on a new design. Fit, both in its tailored form and in its dressmaking variant, is inevitably part of the value of the couture. A designer or her or his trusted fitter will conduct the client through a series of fittings to determine the minute adjustments of the garment to the individual's size and sense of comfort. A client is led carefully through the process by a *vendeuse* who is a highly knowledgeable salesperson.

Haute couture depends upon the projection of a garment that is ideal to the creator's vision and that can be rendered to the specific demands and shape of the client. Charles Frederick Worth established the tradition that set his enterprise apart from dressmaking: he showed collections semiannually, allowing the garments to stand as his aesthetic statement and permitting the client to select from among the designs available. Thus, as one can see in the pages that follow, designers have allowed for the smallest modifications in dressmaking or the calipering of tailoring to adjust a perfect shape to the needs of a human body. Madeleine Vionnet's or Alix Grès's subtlety in dressmaking incorporated into the perfect design the possible adjustments that make the dress suitable to the client. The couture is like architecture, dependent on the synergy between client and architect for realization of a project but always cognizant of landscape and existing physical properties. Similarly, the couture garment is a fulfillment of mutually agreeing ideas that are contingent upon and wrought on the human body.

The essence of tailoring is the simulation of line on the three-dimensional body, while the substance of dressmaking is finding sculptural form in the soft materials of apparel. Tailoring is planar, working with a relatively firm fabric. Dressmaking pertains to the articulation of form from the manipulation of more pliant cloth. Tailoring proceeds from cutting the segments that constitute pattern, whereas dressmaking achieves its effect through draping. While the goals of these techniques are not mutually exclusive, they render two distinct forms of clothing, each capable of meeting the designer's ideal and each capable of perfect calibration to the client.

JEAN-PHILIPPE WORTH

Wedding gown, 1896
Cream silk damask
Gift of Miss Agnes Miles
Carpenter, 1941 (CI 41.14.1)

Employing a textile design that
mirrors itself from selvage to
selvage, Worth created a dress
pieced into a perfectly symmetrical
image at the center. The absorption
of image to hourglass silhouette
further demonstrates Worth's
mastery, as the ultimate dressmaking is constituted in the
smooth, custom-made fit of this
gown. Tiny hand-stitched cartridge
pleats at the shoulder create huge
leg-of-mutton sleeves that offset
the fit, which cleaves to the period's
ideal silhouette of narrow waist
and bell-shaped fullness of
the skirt.

MADELEINE VIONNET

Bias-cut day dress, 1920 (left)
Ecru silk crepe
Gift of Judith Backer Grunberg,
1993 (1993.228)

Bias-cut day dress, ca. 1932 (right)
Ivory silk crepe
Gift of Mrs. T. Reed Vreeland, 1961
(CI 61.3.2)

Even as early as 1920, Vionnet was
working with fabric on a diagonal
grain so it created a supple
skimming over the body. Earlier
silks conformed to the armature
of the fashionable silhouette, but
Vionnet elected to use high-twist
crepe on the bias, exploiting the
fabric's elasticity to express a softness of silhouette and to suggest
the uncorseted body effects that
the designer inaugurated. Vionnet
found ingenious ways to conceal
the critical shaping of a dress—fus-
ing front and back and articulating
principles of the body without
explicit structure—within what
seemed to be only minor devices
of decoration. In the dress on
the right, chevron faggoting in
fine-thread drawnwork creates
arrowheads that reiterate the
direction of the grain.

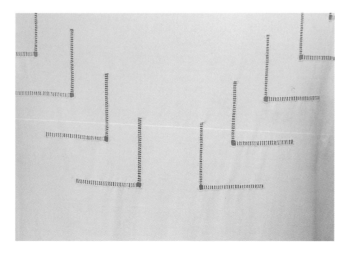

Madeleine Vionnet

Day dress, 1926–27
Maroon silk crepe
Gift of Mrs. Aline Bernstein, 1945
(CI 45.103.2)

The unexpected challenge of couture design in the late 1910s and 1920s was to create forms out of soft fabric without reliance on any underlying structure. It is as if sculpture had been reconstituted from an art of base and mass to an art with legerdemain and supple balances, as it would become over decades. But Vionnet mastered first and most successfully the possibilities of minimal structures imposed on soft fabric to set up a delicate fulcrum of volume and balance. A day dress achieves stability in the dynamic of silk crepe rendered as a lattice, just enough structure in tiny pin tucks to set off differing tensions to the bias (see detail on page 10). Below the lattice, Vionnet created a waist seam to which she attached the finely box-pleated skirt.

Madeleine Vionnet

Cocktail dress, 1936
Black silk organza tucked in a
honeycomb pattern
Gift of Mrs. John Chambers
Hughes, 1958 (CI 58.34.15)

Vionnet offered an ultimate
performance in lithe equilibrium
with a bodice constructed of one
piece, seamed at the waist (see
detail). All shaping is created by the
graduated hexagons. Thus, Vionnet
imposed all form through the illu-
sion of embellishment but carefully
concealed a system of minuscule
adjustments into the design of the
tucking. This sublimated essential
structure is akin to modern architecture's streamlined vocabulary of
ornament to serve compositional
needs.

JEANNE LANVIN

Evening dress, ca. 1930
Light green silk taffeta and
silk net
Gift of Mrs. Jill L. Leinbach
and James L. Long, in memory
of their mother, Mrs. Jane P.
Long, 1986 (1986.377.1a–c)

A silk tulle skirt is obscured
by bias ruffles, bringing the
relatively flat bias construction
of Vionnet to a more three-
dimensional application. Other
bias bands crisscross at the
neckline, joined imperceptibly
to the body of the dress by a
narrow web of tulle.

ALIX GRÈS

Dinner dress, ca. 1939 (left)
Pink silk jersey
Gift of Mrs. John A. van Beuren
and Mrs. Samuel M. V. Hamilton,
1977 (1977.210.21)

LUCIEN LELONG

Dinner dress, spring 1940 (right)
Pale turquoise silk jersey with
gold embroidered belt
Gift of Bettina Ballard, 1958
(CI 58.7.7a,b)

By the 1930s, use of bias had
become a convention of evening
wear. Alix used a fine-gauge silk
jersey to achieve liquid bias-like
effects, often with reference to
the "wet" drapery of classical
sculpture. Alix's implied classi-
cism accorded to the period's
interest in Greek and Roman
examples for theater, poetry, and
the visual arts. While Alix
designed in circumstances sug-
gesting the isolation of an artist's
studio, Lelong surrounded him-
self with assistants of individual
talent. He served as springboard
for many young designers: the
1940 dress is said to be by Dior.

MAINBOCHER

Wedding dress of the Duchess of Windsor, 1937
Dove gray (originally blue)
silk crepe
Gift of the Duchess of Windsor,
1950 (CI 50.110a–d)

Mainbocher was known for his
sense of decorum, creating a
garment impeccable to and proper
for the occasion. If there was a reti-
cence to his design, as opposed to
the modern experiments of others
in the 1930s, it was because he
sought an unerring gentility. Decoration was held to a minimum,
and Mainbocher favored refined
feminine forms (petal-shaped collar,
shirring, small embroideries; see
detail on page 116). Even the gloves
were specifically designed to
accommodate the wedding ring.
While, due to a defect in the stability of the dye, the dress has
uniformly lost its "Windsor blue,"
it retains the willful seemliness of a
marriage in world view.

JACQUES GRIFFE

Cocktail dress, spring 1951
Gunmetal silk organza
Gift of Mrs. Byron C. Foy, 1953
(CI 53.40.14a–f)

Griffe, who had worked with
Vionnet, permitted the graduated
structural elements to become
ornament. Far more grandiloquent
than Vionnet and, in the manner
of the 1950s, returning to crinoline-
like shaping and picturesque
resplendence in fashion, Griffe created a full skirt with welt tucks that
encase bands of horsehair. One
feature of this period is that the
horsehair progresses very subtly
from narrow to wider, demonstrat-
ing the sophisticated resources of
the couture. Arguably, every skill
of the couture flourished in the
1950s, and dresses seem to celebrate
the métiers in an almost self-
conscious flamboyance.

HUBERT DE GIVENCHY

Day dress, ca. 1967 (left)
Oatmeal wool tweed double knit
Gift of Diana Vreeland, 1979
(1979.435.9a,b)

Day dress, 1963–67 (right)
Oatmeal wool tweed double knit
Gift of Diana Vreeland, 1979
(1979.435.10a,b)

The relaxed attitudes of the 1960s
could be achieved in couture day
wear. Hubert de Givenchy excelled
in a style associated with such non-
chalant style paladins as Jacqueline
Kennedy Onassis and Audrey
Hepburn. Learning from his men-
tor, Balenciaga, Givenchy offered a
seemingly unstructured two-piece
dress indebted to the Balenciaga
sack, and dubbed his "split level."
For necessary articulation of
details, he employed "souplesse"
instead of a tailor's dart, allowing a
supplementary soft fold of material
to give shape to these unassuming
and chic tops.

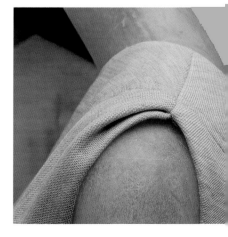

MADAME (ALIX) GRÈS

Evening gown, 1958
White silk jersey
Gift of Mrs. Leon L. Roos, 1973 (1973.104.2)

Grès, working earlier as Alix, created dresses in shafts
of fabrics, the divers fluting of which served as a body
entasis like the architectural model of a classical column.
Seaming together fabric vertically to be continuous from
hem to neckline, Grès pleated and tucked the materials
into a shaping suitable to the body: the same fabric is
buoyant and fluid when release-pleated from the waist
down; Grès simulated a waist seam by tight tucking that
continues through the bodice; and she crowned the dress
with volutes and twists that extend the same fabric that
is so liquid and ample at the bottom. This tour de force
of material rendered in diverse ways accounts for the
tempered ergonomics of such dresses. Their wearers have
testified that they felt secure and not immodest in these
dresses, so organic was their creation. In this dress, only
one piece of fabric was added to the column: as seen in
the detail, a small triangle was inserted under the arm to
complete the structure, but otherwise the entire dress is
conceived as one cylinder.

CRISTOBAL BALENCIAGA

Evening ensemble, ca. 1962
Moss green Indian sari silk with
woven gold trim
Gift of Mrs. Ephraim London, 1994
(1994.573a,b)

A loyal client provided Balenciaga
with an Indian sari and asked
the designer to create a dress.
Balenciaga rendered couture technique to the flat textile, cutting
apart the woven edging and
appliquéing it to form a border for
the whole of the garment. In this
way, he respected the Indian source
but addressed the textile as if it
were a couture fabric.

India, and in particular the tradition of the sari, had long captivated
the West. Bias draping of the 1920s
and 1930s was influenced by the
sari. That Balenciaga pursued the
idea in the 1960s is late evidence of
this long tradition.

CHANEL
BY KARL LAGERFELD

Evening gown and cape,
spring/summer 1995
Red silk chiffon
Courtesy Chanel

In a hand-stitched shirring worthy
of Vionnet or Grès, needle and
thread are passed through to create
fine gathers for both a cape and a
gown. Structure is discovered in
technical prowess. No further decoration is necessary beyond that
inherent in the process of making
the dress. In this, Lagerfeld
demonstrates one of his special
preoccupations of allowing the
couture process to become the form
of the garment, an idea akin to
contemporary art.

GABRIELLE CHANEL

Day ensemble, ca. 1927
Pink and black floral-printed silk
chiffon and beige wool tweed
Isabel Shults Fund, 1984
(1984.31a–c)

Chanel excelled in soft tailoring.
This particular coat-and-dress
ensemble blends dressmaker
techniques with the definite
finishes of the tailor. The fabric is
reinforced with ornamental over-
stitching in a manner which,
seeming decoration, is structural
trussing. In fact, this soft tailoring
became the token of the Chanel
suit in the designer's sustained
evolution until her death in 1971.

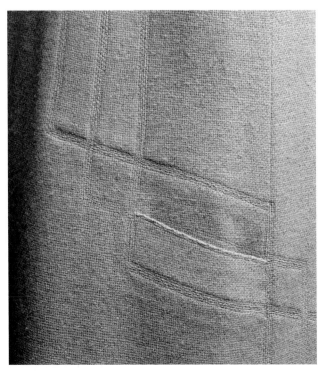

PIERRE CARDIN

Day suit, ca. 1960 (left)
Gold wool tweed
Gift of Kay Kerr Uebel, 1994 (1994.164.2a,b)

This suit demonstrates Cardin's penchant for creating dramatic form from cloth. He extended the conventions of strict tailoring to incorporate a soft peplum with a controlled gathering that reveals his understanding of the balance and grain of fabric. His predisposition to an architectonic approach is evident in his shoulder and sleeve treatment. Cardin's innovation in the 1950s was his ability to think in terms both of fashion subtlety and semaphore, seeking the graphic emblem without vitiating the qualities of tailoring.

PIERRE CARDIN

Day coat, fall 1966 (facing page)
Plum wool
Gift of Mrs. Charles Wrightsman, 1968 (CI 68.78.5)

One of the first designers to embrace a futuristic geometry, Cardin referenced fashion to contemporary dress and to an ideal of clothing for the future. He offered a streamlined future that was, in the post-Sputnik epoch, inflected by science fiction and a quixotic dream of Space-Age technology and amelioration. The diamond-shaped gusset at the waist reflects a treatment of cloth that began with Vionnet.

CRISTOBAL BALENCIAGA

Day coat, 1961
Pale gray-green brushed wool
Gift of Estate of Ann E. Woodward,
1987 (1987.349.4a,b)

Of all twentieth-century designers,
said Chanel, the only one who could
create a garment from beginning
to end was Balenciaga. His compre-
hensive mastery is indicated in
understanding of fabric and in his
awareness that a wide wedge-shaped
coat could become in final appear-
ance a cinched silhouette, playing
with grain and incorporating ease.

LANVIN
BY CLAUDE MONTANA

Suit, spring/summer 1990
Turquoise blue wool, black wool
gabardine
Courtesy Josie Natori

Montana, a ready-to-wear designer
recruited to the couture by Lanvin,
is noted for his aggressive imposi-
tion of edifice-like forms on the
body. He seems to create a Le
Corbusier structure in dress. When
Montana worked with a couture
atelier, he emphasized his interest
in tailoring, but with seemingly
simple effects that could only be
accomplished by the most skilled
hands.

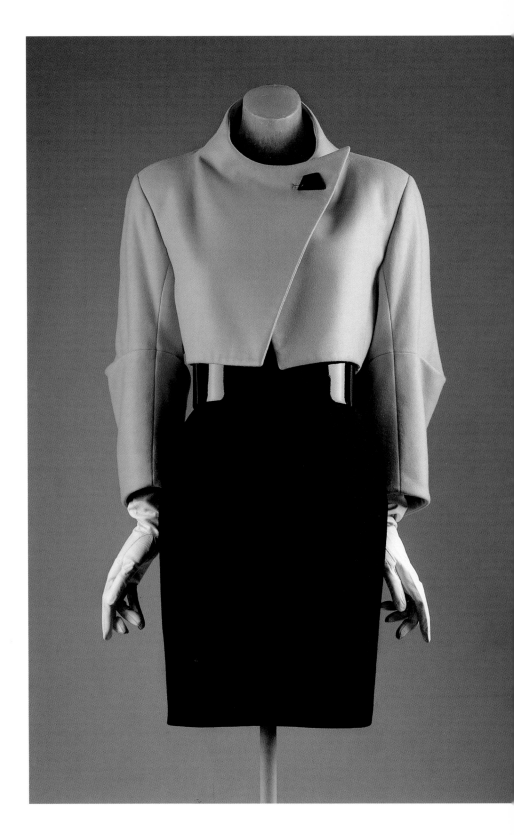

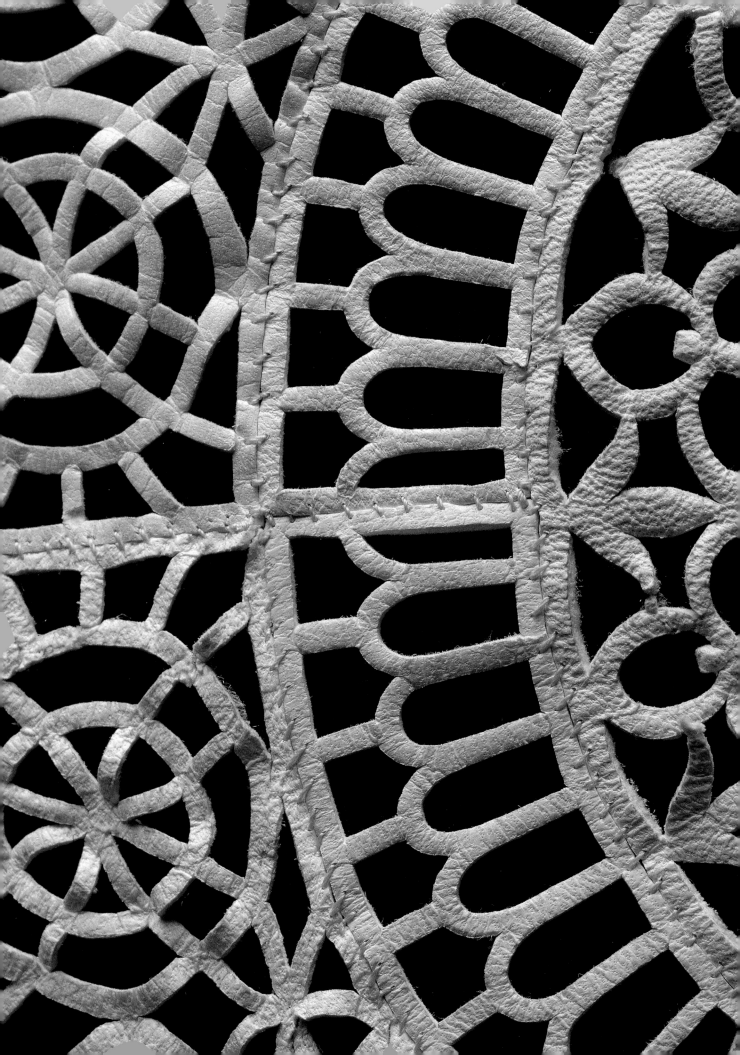

TECHNIQUE

The work of Diderot to delineate the *métiers* in the service of dress anticipates their continuing role in the emerging couture houses of the mid-nineteenth century. Outside the *maisons de couture,* governed by the designers, stand the many ateliers of specialized fashion trades that constitute essential elements of the couture. We have chosen to indicate only the *métiers* that are applied directly onto the garment. The fully accessorized and complemented wearing of the couture depends, of course, upon a large corps of ancillary makers: glovers, costume jewelers, enamel and nacre workers, milliners, hairdressers, shoemakers, and furriers. As master embroiderer François Lesage pointed out, "the humble 'tradesmen's entrance' opens straight onto the red carpet leading to the heights of haute couture." These are not trades and *métiers* as mere competencies of toil. They are, as Diderot catalogued and reasoned for an uncertain heritage, the enabling arts and veritable gifts of the couture.

Workshop masteries distinguish the couture from other visual arts. Embroidery that can make a fictive display of jewelry on a dress or re-create a painting onto clothing, and featherwork that improves upon nature in articulating the shape of each feather provide the couture with an absolute control founded in ancient crafts. The long dynamic of the relationship between the couture specialists and the couture designers has been that the designers often set tasks that might seem to challenge the possibilities of the *métier* medium, but that yield a tour de force accomplishment. In fact, a sample from the lace maker or embroiderer may often be the source of inspiration to the designer. One cannot imagine Schiaparelli independent of Lesage embroidery or Lanvin without the tradition of Lemarié featherwork.

When Lucien Lelong, president of the Chambre Syndicale during the War, was challenged by the Nazi authorities to transport the couture to Berlin in the 1940s, he responded that such a move was impossible because of the synergy between the couturiers and the *petites mains* workshops. To have taken the couture to Berlin would have meant moving hundreds of ateliers, and so the führer's plan was thwarted.

Detail of Poiret coat (see page 76)

Paris has remained the epicenter of the couture since the time of Worth, not because of an obdurate nationalism but because of an abiding tradition of creative resources, human and physical. Designers from elsewhere in the world have entered the couture as a practice and profession, respecting Paris as its heart. Even as the couture changes in sensibilities from flamboyance to elegant restraint, as in our time, or from using the familiar materials to new technical experiments, the practice of luxury remains sustained by the hand skills that speak, in themselves, of mastery, subtlety, and etiquette.

What distinguishes the couture garment from a ready-to-wear piece is the handwork, functioning not as luxe augmentation, but as a capability intrinsic to the garment. Thus, the embroidery, lace, and feathers of the following pages are not after-the-fact decorations that finish the garments but their enabling principles, the elements of creation that are the matrix of the design process. Even though practiced outside the *maisons de couture,* the work of Diderot's old *métiers* is inherent in the designs of the haute couture.

JEAN-PHILIPPE WORTH

Ball gown, 1900–1905
Ice blue silk satin embroidered in scrolling floral motif
Gift of Mrs. Walter H. Page, 1979 (1979.251.4a,b)

Jean-Philippe Worth succeeded his father as designer
for the House of Worth, creating to great favor the stiff-
ened, slightly archaic, rococo revival of the turn of the
century. The house continued its virtuoso technical
achievements, as represented in this example, in which
metallic thread is couched to render baskets and scrolling
ribbons, and ivory marquisette is cut into circles and
pulled in at the perimeter to make the soft three-
dimensional petals that are then applied to the fabric. As
the twentieth century began, these designs recalled the
eighteenth century, but even more importantly their
crafts and artisanal opulence implied the conservative
impulse of the couture opposed to the novelties of a
new era.

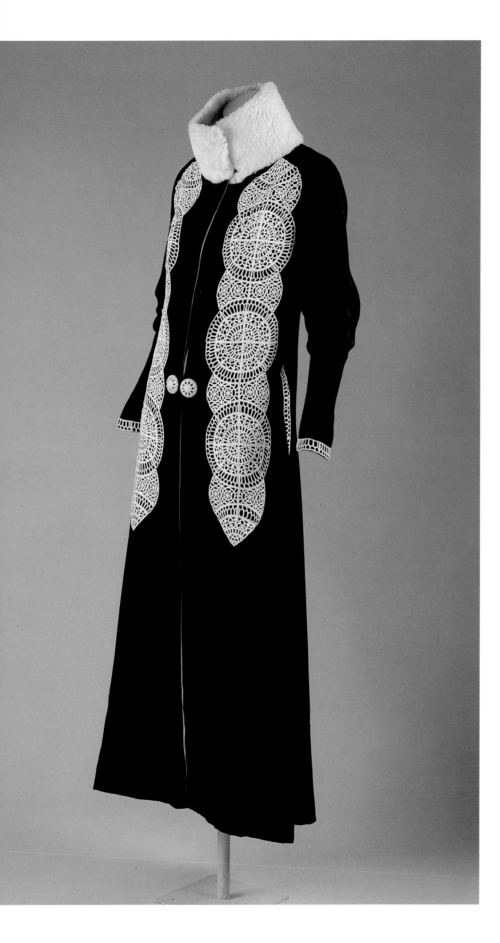

PAUL POIRET

Coat, ca. 1919
Black silk and wool blend with
white leather appliqués and
white fur trim
Gift of Mrs. David J. Colton, 1961
(CI 61.40.4)

In the 1910s, Poiret introduced an
avant-garde sensibility into the
couture. His penchant for the opulent gesture, lusher fabrics, fur, and
feathers was part of his grandiose
Gesamtkunstwerk, inspired by
stage and Orientalist extravaganza.
He was also capable of more sub-
dued garments. In the case of this
day coat with leather appliqués, the
leather is cut into a delicate filigree
and couched by hand onto the wool
to create a graphic lattice of white
over black (see detail on page 72).
The cylindrical silhouette and
standing collar suggest inspiration
from Chinese or Near Eastern robes
and coats.

JEANNE LANVIN

Dinner dress, ca. 1924
Ivory hammered silk satin with black silk satin appliqués
Gift of Mrs. Carter Marshall Braxton, 1980
(1980.92.1a–c)

Seeking in both the new cylindrical silhouettes and in
her characteristic robes de style to adorn flat planes with
the new designs associated with Art Deco, Lanvin devel-
oped a repertoire of motifs at once modern and decorative. Black cutouts are stitched by hand to a contrasting
white dress. The design is even further integrated into
the dress by the stitching's being hidden under the edge
of the appliqué, thus making it appear a pieced rather
than an applied patterning.

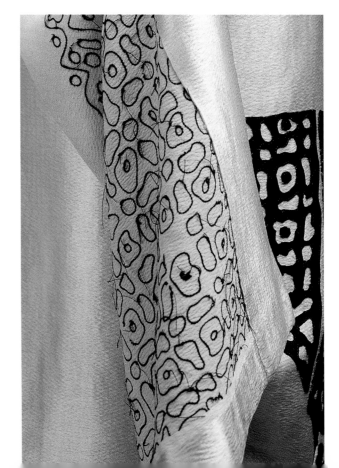

JEANNE LANVIN

Robe de style, summer 1924
Black silk taffeta with green silk and sequin
embroidered medallions and silver corded net
Gift of Mrs. Albert Spalding, 1962 (CI 62.58.1)

Chinoiserie roundels that intimate the most
elaborate past of the Chinese court, alternately
resembling embroidered Manchu court badge
motifs or the glinting scales of Mongol armor
interpreted in Western embroidery, animate a robe
de style by Lanvin. Dabbling with the ambience of
historicisms, heavy with paillettes and beads,
Lanvin also introduces a play with gravity, mingling
the apparently heavy and weightless. A folded layer
of ivory silk tulle that has been corded with silver
metallic thread suggests the rainbow hem of a
Manchu robe.

JEAN PATOU

Evening dress, ca. 1927
Off-white silk charmeuse
embroidered with colored beads
and gold sequins
Gift of Mrs. John A. van Beuren
and Mrs. Samuel M. V. Hamilton,
1977 (1977.210.16)

While Chanel has become the
remembered name, in the 1920s
Jean Patou was as important as
Gabrielle Chanel in introducing
ideas of the new woman
sponsored by sports vigor and
design simplicity. His dresses
were designed with a post–World
War I ideal in mind: woman
enfranchised and empowered. In
particular, Patou held the New
World as a model of the new
woman. He imported a cohort of
American women to serve as
mannequins; even his evening
wear had the simplicity of a
tennis shift and depended on
its elaborate embroidery as sole
improvement on the mechanics
of sportswear.

ELSA SCHIAPARELLI

Evening ensemble, 1937 (left)
Dark green satin-backed crepe
gown, dark green silk velvet
jacket with gold tinsel and bead
embroidery
Gift of Julia B. Henry, 1978
(1978.288.19a–c)

Evening jacket, 1938 (right)
Plum red silk crepe with sequin
and bead embroidery
Gift of Mrs. J. R. Keagy, 1974
(1974.338.2)

Introducing sinister and Surrealist-
inspired themes to the arts of
embroidery, Schiaparelli created
an art of conceptualism and con-
cupiscence. Cicada buttons are a
decoration of equivocal or complex
beauty as are Schiaparelli's flowers
in "amber." Known for collabora-
tions with Salvador Dali and Jean
Cocteau, Schiaparelli was also
capable of creating her own idio-
syncratic Surrealism independent
of these artists.

MADELEINE VIONNET

Evening gown, summer 1938
Pale gray-blue crepe completely
embroidered with rows of fringe
in scallop motif
Gift of Madame Madeleine
Vionnet, 1952 (CI 52.18.4)

Though there are separate specialists for applied braid and fringe,
known as the *crépinières,* Vionnet
has chosen in this instance to em-
ploy an embroidery of individual
graduated lengths of silk thread
passed and looped through the
fabric, with each thread forming
two drops of fringe. The scallop
arcs constitute the sole decoration
of the dress.

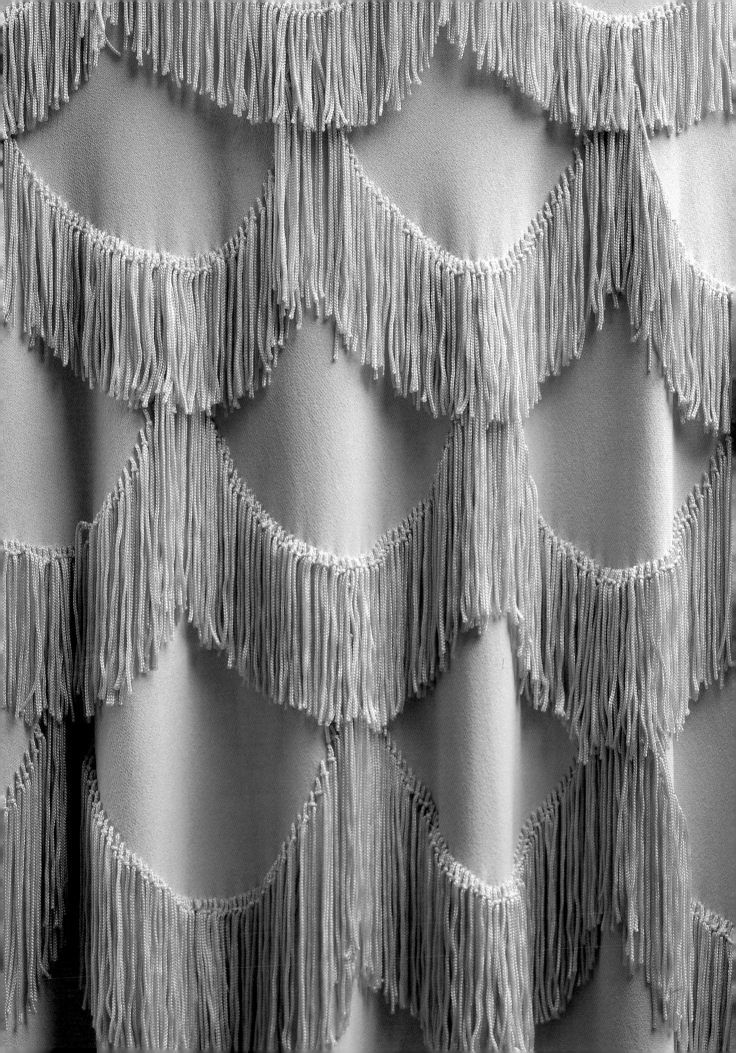

ELSA SCHIAPARELLI

Evening cape, 1938
Black silk velvet embroidered
with gold sequins in a design
inspired by the Neptune
Fountain in the Parc de
Versailles
Bequest of Lady Mendl, 1951
(CI 51.83)

In an instance of sui generis
pertinence to one client, a velvet
cape for Lady Mendl refers to
her propensities for the spectac-
ular and the eighteenth century
and celebrates the Neptune
Fountain and its proximity to
her house in the Parc de
Versailles. Schiaparelli's own interest in the eighteenth century
is evident in her jacket (see
frontispiece) with glass embroidered rococo hand mirrors
bracketing buttons cast as
Hellenic deities.

JACQUES FATH

Ball gown, ca. 1952
Black silk velvet with ivory silk
satin, white mink, and gold
metal trim
Gift of Mrs. Giorgio Uzielli, 1984
(1984.606.3a,b)

Known for flattering dinner dresses
that set off the head and shoulders
with an audacious décolletage, Fath
created a cantilevered outer bodice
with a modest ivory satin under-
bodice. The extended plane of the
outer bodice is like the soaring
shapes of Saarinen buildings, estab-
lishing an artifice within the canon
of modernist restraint. Fath played
with the contrast—of matte and
shiny, of ivory and black, of white
fur and gold bullion—as a rich
textural perimeter for the dress.

CHRISTIAN DIOR

Ball gown, ca. 1952 (left)
White silk organza embroidered with allover pattern of grasses and clover
Gift of Mrs. David Kluger, 1960 (CI 60.21.1a,b)

Cocktail dress, spring 1952 (right)
White silk organza heavily embroidered with a floral motif
Gift of Mrs. Byron C. Foy, 1955 (CI 55.76.20a–d)

The designer set exacting tasks for his embroiderer, Rebé. The embroidery is set in a nuanced spacing of elements with the densest application at the waist, thinning as it falls away to the hem. This seemingly organic application, simulating a diminishment in nature, is further enhanced by Rebé's repertoire of embroidery stitches to create a dimensionality of the surface. The effect is optically then like a meadow's variegation.

CHRISTIAN DIOR

"Junon" ball gown, fall 1949 (left)
Pale blue silk net embroidered with
iridescent sequins
Gift of Mrs. Byron C. Foy, 1953
(CI 53.40.5a–e)

"Venus" ball gown, fall 1949 (right)
Gray silk net embroidered with
feather-shaped opalescent sequins
Gift of Mrs. Byron C. Foy, 1953
(CI 53.40.7a–e)

Rebé embroidery, more than that
of any other embroidery house,
evinced a fine eighteenth-century
sensibility compatible with Dior's
profound longing for the past.
Only four years after World War II,
the artisanal trades had fully
recovered, rendering to the
couture materials and applications
as rich as before. As Dior restored a
grand silhouette, he also reinstated
artisanal luxury. Even the most
subtle molded nacreous paillettes
and graduated sequins were available and were used by Dior.

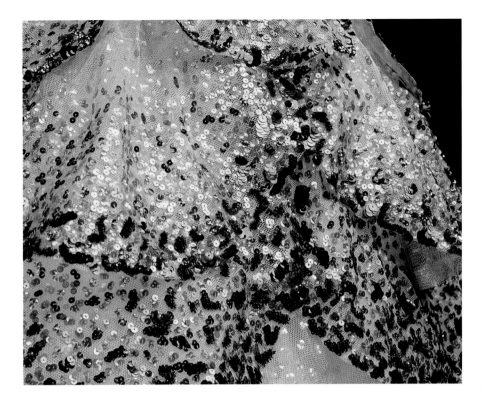

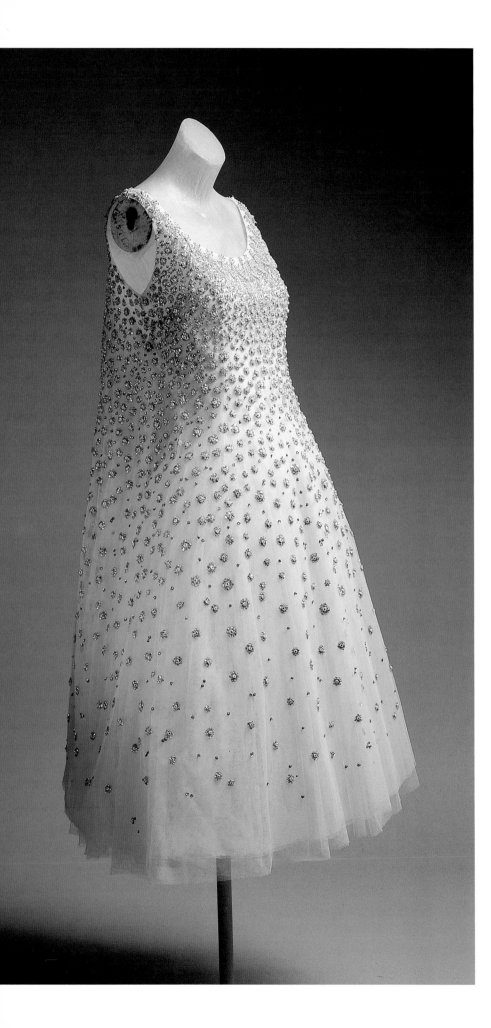

CHRISTIAN DIOR
BY YVES SAINT LAURENT

"L'Éléphant blanc" evening dress,
spring/summer 1958
White silk net embroidered with
silver thread and rhinestones
Gift of Bernice Chrysler Garbisch,
1977 (1977.329.5)

Creating the trapeze silhouette for
Dior, Saint Laurent has a rigid
understructure veiled under a fly-
away cage. A boned corset anchors
the dress but allows the delusion
of a free-swinging cone. Seeking a
shape for independence, though
still tethered, the "Éléphant Blanc"
dress also employs a shimmering
embroidery on net that requires
a finishing flourish to the thread
work on a transparent surface.
Thus, in both surface decoration
and in structure, Saint Laurent
gained the effect of ethereal,
buoyant freedom while retain-
ing the structure of the couture.
From the earliest works at the
house of Dior through the designer's accomplishments in his
own house, Saint Laurent has practiced and perfected this modernist
wielding of couture construction
and proficiency to seem wholly
unfettered.

HUBERT DE GIVENCHY

Evening gown, 1963
Coral cotton lace reembroidered with coral-colored beads and coral pieces
Gift of Mrs. John Hay Whitney, 1974 (1974.184.2)

Coral with matching glass beads is applied in high relief on the armature of a minimalist Givenchy silhouette. A princess-seam dress skimming the torso, but flaring to the hem, is almost severe, but it is rendered rococo and ornate by the surface treatment. Givenchy's special trait was to find an equilibrium between excess and the reductive. An austere form supports a heavily encrusted embroidery, making a gown that works both as an extravagance and as a spartan design.

YVES SAINT LAURENT

"Crocodile" evening jacket, 1986
Blue sequin and seed bead embroidered silk and
royal blue silk satin
Courtesy Yves Saint Laurent

The new embroidery devised by François Lesage for
Saint Laurent sets off large jewel-like sequins anchored
at an angle in order to form the dimensional effects of
the scaling of a crocodile against the inflection of small
seed beads. The platelet sequins are hand-colored to
emphasize the deepness of the relief.

YVES SAINT LAURENT

Evening dress, 1983
Silver and brown sequin and seed
bead embroidered silk
Courtesy Yves Saint Laurent

Pushing embroidery from a
decorative device of the surface to
a place of structural conceit, Saint
Laurent uses the embroiderer's
skill to obliterate all the seaming
required for a skintight fit. Refer-
encing the naiad, or even the fish
itself (sometimes known as the
sardine dress), Saint Laurent had
a prototype in nature, but his penchant is always for the artifice, the
supreme creation that in this case
is the integrity of the dress that
appears indivisible, yet flexible and
formfitting. Made to the client, the
couture always offers a perfect fit;
Saint Laurent hyperbolizes even
the couture to create the dress as
an iridescent skin.

Chanel
by Karl Lagerfeld

Evening suit, fall/winter 1986–87
Black sequin, gold seed bead,
and black chenille embroidered
black silk
Courtesy Chanel

In embroidery that simulates the
interior quilting of a classic Chanel
jacket, Lagerfeld makes a clever
allusion to Coco Chanel. In making
conspicuous the Chanel chain and
quilting, Lagerfeld takes the secrets
of the couture for granted and
flaunts his relationship to the past.
The quilted surface and a binding
resembling a black corded gold
chain in seed beads and sequins
render iconic the devices of classic
Chanel and render ironic the capa-
bilities of the new master of the
legacy.

CHANEL
BY KARL LAGERFELD

Evening gown, fall/winter 1995–96
Black silk ribbon embroidered net
Courtesy Chanel

Not only does silk ribbon create a
dense meander within a field of silk
net, but it is attached in a way that
stands it on edge, making the net
demonstrably three dimensional, as
if it were a cage of continuous silk
ribbon. Flattened, a ribbon encased
in an embroidery screen could be
relatively inert. The effect here
(seen especially in detail, page 8)
is both spidery and as animated in
painting-sculpture dilemma as a
Frank Stella wall sculpture.

CHANEL BY KARL LAGERFELD

Evening ensemble, spring/summer 1995
White and blue-black seed bead embroidered silk satin
and black silk chiffon
Courtesy Chanel

Lagerfeld offers the deliberate paradox of a sailor's
sweater from vernacular dress rendered in the luxury
of couture. The designer's zeal for common clothing
and popular themes, especially for the house of Chanel,
where the acumen about menswear and practical
clothing has always prevailed, does not vitiate his
commitment to the excellence in design and technique of
the couture. On the contrary, it is as if the juxtaposition
of the two polar levels of fashion refines the couture's
virtues and stimulates the couture's imagination.

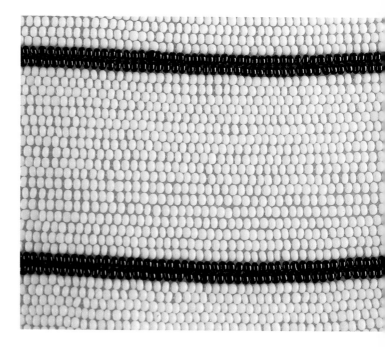

GABRIELLE CHANEL

Evening gown, 1936
White Chantilly lace and silk net
Gift of Mrs. Stephen M. Kellen,
1978 (1978.165.16a,b)

Silk net has been treated in a labor-
intensive manner with ruffles
shirred in, set by heat, and the
shirring thread removed. Designer
of no-nonsense and men's-
tailoring-inspired sportswear,
Chanel was not oblivious to the
beautiful benefits of the virtuoso
hand-sewn details of the couture.
If Vionnet was, in the 1920s and
1930s, the chief designer of configuration achieved through delicate
but strategic hand sewing, Chanel
was nonetheless aware of how
much form could be achieved by
the smallest stitch, even in this
case with the thread subsequently
removed.

MADELEINE VIONNET

Evening gown, 1939
Black cotton lace with velvet appliqués
over silver lamé
Gift of Mrs. Harrison Williams, 1952
(CI 52.24.2a,b)

A bias lamé underdress is visible through
the veil of a lace overdress with velvet.
Seeking the unity of the garment and the
integrity of cloth, Vionnet found simplifi-
cation even in lace, adding only a small
panel at the waist to the one-piece bodice.
Thus, even in the sheerest and inherently
particled garment, Vionnet insisted on the
largest possible element.

YVES SAINT LAURENT

Evening ensemble, spring 1963
Reappliquéd white silk organdy guipure
Gift of Mrs. Charles Wrightsman, 1964 (CI 64.59.7a,b)

The patron saint of lace makers is Saint Anne, mother of Mary. Maternal and feminine, immaculate and important, the traditions of lace making have been associated for centuries with the finest in dress. Lace embellishments to court dress for both men and women were evidence of power displayed through a craft. Hand-appliquéd lace defies the machine aesthetic and convenience in as palpable a form as any. The white-on-white relief of guipure is a small allover sculpture articulating the surface of a very modest, even elementary, silhouette. Saint Laurent knows that ethereal handcraft garniture is most effective when combined with an unpretentious modern structure.

GIANNI VERSACE

Evening dress,
fall/winter 1991–92 (left)
Pink quilted silk satin,
silk georgette, lace
Gift of Versace, 1993 (1993.53.1)

Evening dress,
fall/winter 1991–92 (right)
Pale blue quilted silk satin,
silk georgette, lace
Gift of Versace, 1993 (1993.53.2)

Setting the most complex and
concentrated tasks for the expertise
of the couture ateliers, Versace
brings satin in trapunto into imme-
diate conjunction with pleated lace.
Lace is customarily a flat panel;
Versace delights in applying a
second unexpected effect upon
one technical privilege of the
couture. Always inclined, even in
his ready-to-wear, to challenge the
possibilities of the medium,
Versace's couture work summons
its own tests of technique.

LOUISEBOULANGER
Evening dress, 1928
Gray-beige silk satin with
ostrich-feather trim
Gift of Mrs. Wolcott Blair, 1973
(1973.6)

Feathers of the 1920s swayed with
the new music and dance, benefited
from Orientalism's panache and
bent for the exotic, and allowed
clothing to be more fluid and
flexible than ever. Here, the feather
trim is individual filaments of
ostrich plume knotted together to
form longer strands. Each segment
is dyed a different tone for the
effect of an ombré cascade. The
feather in nature is a beautiful
form, but Louiseboulanger's
feathers are purposely governed
and distilled beyond natural beauty
to achieve a trim synthetic and
sophisticated.

HUBERT DE GIVENCHY

Evening gown, ca. 1968
Salmon-colored silk with feathers
Gift of Mrs. Claus von Bülow, 1971
(1971.79.4)

The feathers of this dress are
stripped down to the tip to create
an artificial profile. Indicative of
the couture in seeking an
improvement even on nature,
these contrived feathers elaborate
on the feather's natural shaping to
create a self-conscious artifice.
The shorter feathers have been
anchored into a scallop pattern that
overlaps to imitate a scale or coat in
nature, but there is no element left
to chance or to nature's careless-
ness. The longer plumes are affixed
at the stem to be tremblant and
animated on the dress.

HUBERT DE GIVENCHY

Evening dress, ca. 1966 (left)
Dark brown silk broadcloth with
ostrich feathers
Gift of Bernice Chrysler Garbisch,
1977 (1977.108.3a–c)

CRISTOBAL BALENCIAGA

Evening gown, fall 1965 (right)
Pink dotted silk tulle with
ostrich feathers
Gift of Mrs. Charles Wrightsman,
1966 (CI 66.54.5)

Shaved ostrich feathers, their
filaments stripped and dyed, are
individually applied to the silk,
anchored upward and against the
grain in order to form an animated
field in soft colors. Like the optical
effect of an Impressionist painting,
the dress is seen distinctly at a
distance, but as a complex accretion
at close range.

Hubert de Givenchy

Evening dress, early 1960s
White silk satin and pink net
embroidered with pink crystals
and feathers
Gift of Mrs. John Hay Whitney,
1974 (1974.184.1a–c)

Combining elaborately couched
silver and crystal embroidery with
a fringe of ostrich filaments and individually glued feathers, Givenchy
created a tiered register of luxurious forms. The proximity of
exceptional textures enriches the
waist of the gown. In the lushness
of the overblouse and its pendant
feathers, Givenchy created an
uncertain placement of the waist,
even while directing our attention
to this zone.

YVES SAINT LAURENT

Evening dress, 1969–70
Bird of paradise feathers over beige
silk organza
Gift of Baron Philippe de
Rothschild, 1983 (1983.619.1a,b)

Saint Laurent showed respect for
the natural beauty of the feathers
but created a new beauty as each
has been hand stitched to a nude
organza base. The dress then is the
gossamer creation both airy and
aery, a rara avis of creativity.

CHRISTIAN DIOR
BY GIANFRANCO FERRÉ

Evening coat, 1991
Black and white Mongolian goat
and ostrich feathers
Courtesy Iris Barrel Apfel,
Attata Foundation

Mongolian goat is augmented by
curled and uncurled black-and-
white ostrich feathers. The first impression is of a mottled uniformity,
but the eye becomes attracted to
the greater painterly complexity
of organic materials rendered into
artifice.

CHANEL
BY KARL LAGERFELD

Evening dress, fall/winter 1995–96
Black silk chiffon, Lycra spandex,
stripped black feathers
Courtesy Chanel

In this example, each feather is split
in half down the central quill and
twisted to form spidery ellipses,
incommensurate with any in nature's aviary, more kinetic than the
feather in the wild. What Lagerfeld
discovers in the feather is the
essence of the feather's coil, coat,
kinesis, but each in its Platonic
pith. Nature is surpassed in these
enhanced feathers, deliberately
overstated, especially in the context
of the other filmy and stretchy
textures of the dress.

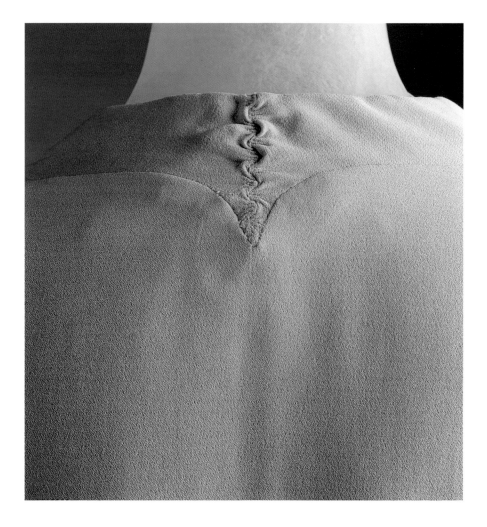

Detail of Mainbocher wedding dress for the Duchess of Windsor (see page 57)

INDEX OF DESIGNERS